When Colorado was Kansas:
Letters from 1859

Check out

Kent Brooks other titles available at

Amazon.com &

Lonesomeprairie.com:

Old Boston: As Wild As They Come

Letters from Colorado: 1880-1889

Letters from Wyoming: 1880-1889

Letters from Nebraska: 1880-1889

Letters from Indian Territory: 1880-1888

Cattle & Cowboys: Letters & More from the 1880s

Letters from Wyoming 1870-1879

Cover: Montgomery, Park County, Colorado, is a group of log dwellings at the base of steep mountain slopes. Grass and standing water are in the foreground. This silver boom town began in 1859, and was abandoned by 1868.[1]

When Colorado Was Kansas:

Letters from 1859

The Heading West Series

Compiled and Annotated

By

Kent Brooks

Kent Brooks

2019

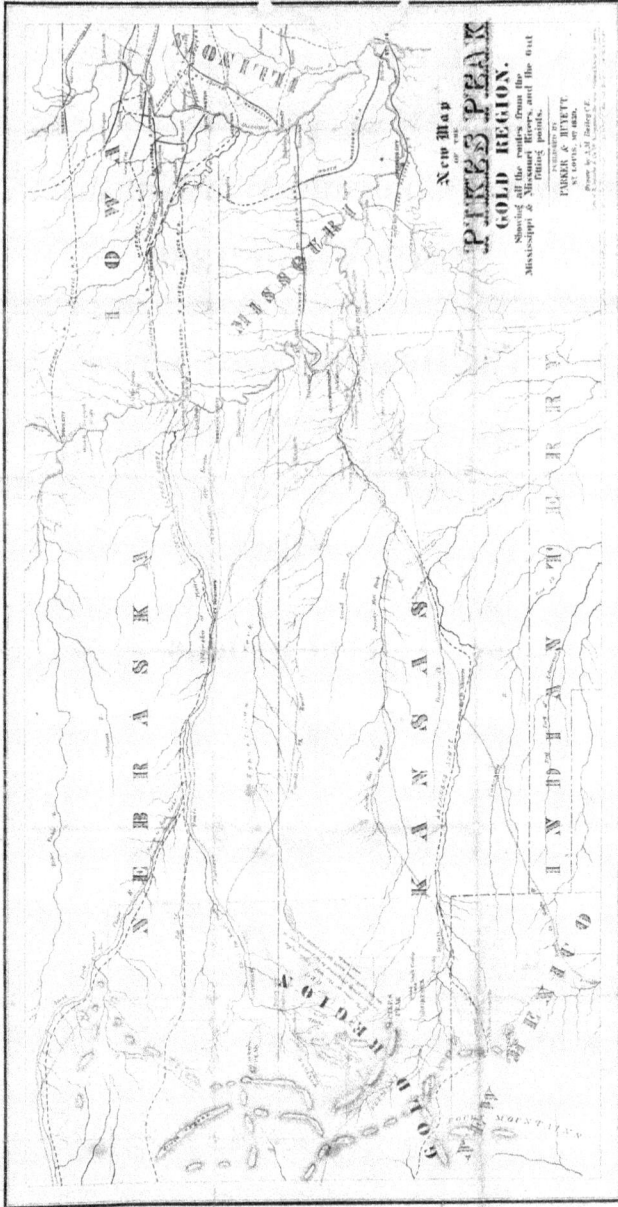

Map of the Pike's Peak gold region, showing all the routes from the
Mississippi and Missouri Rivers, and the Outfitting points.[2]

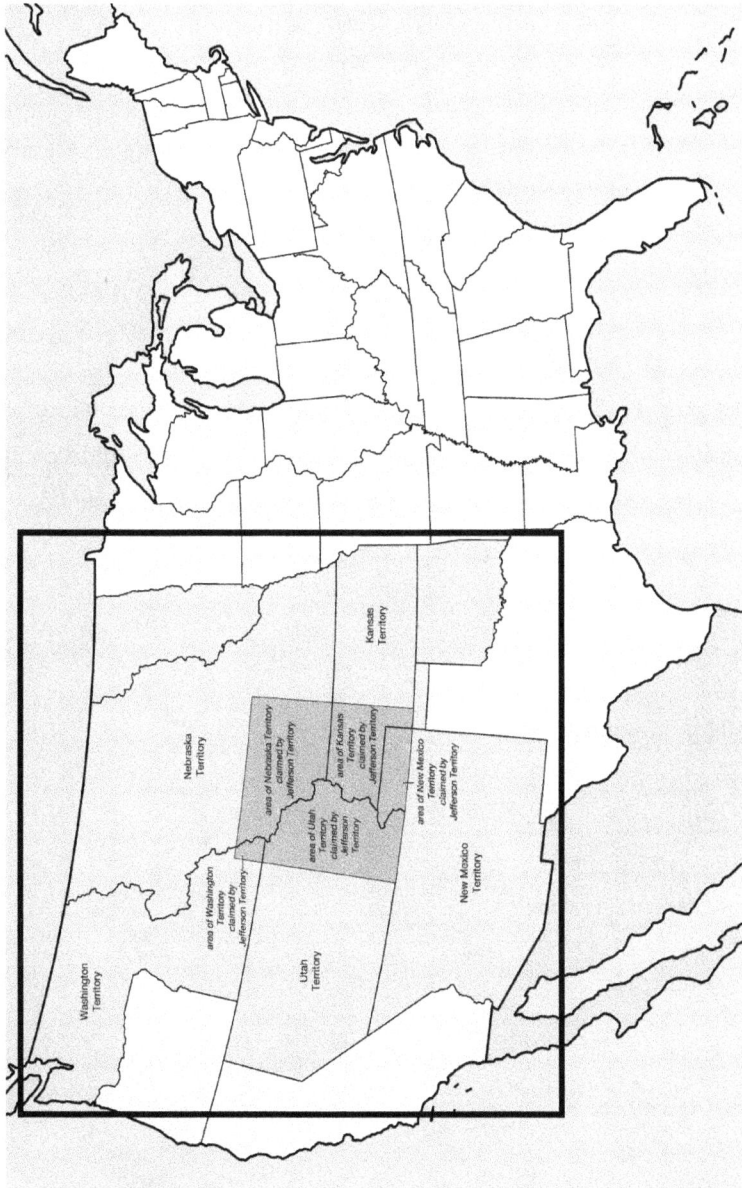

November 7, 1859; Representatives from remote areas of the territories of Kansas, Nebraska, New Mexico, Utah and Washington, form Jefferson Territory. It is never recognized by the federal government but generally governs the area. [3]

First Printing: 2019

ISBN 978-1-7338608-3-3

Lonesome Prairie Publications
PO Box 842
Casper, WY 82601

www.lonesomeprairie.com

Ordering Information:

Special discounts are available on quantity purchases by corporations, associations, educators, and others. For details, contact the publisher at the above listed address.

To the hardy pioneers of old who traveled on foot, on horses, in wagons, via rail and any other means they could to settle the American West. Through the "pen pictures" painted in these letters, you get an unfiltered, first-person account of what they saw when they came to this new place.

Contents

Acknowledgements

The idea and initial content for this work originate from the research I did for my book, "Old Boston: As Wild As They Come." Thanks to the historians of old who didn't have access to the resources available today. I appreciate their work more than ever. I can't imagine putting this project together with a typewriter and without access to digital archives which are available today.

Thank you Lexi-Shae Art for the Book Cover. It is fabulous.

A special thank you goes out to the Denver Public Library, Western History Photographic Collection. Their contribution of photos to this work is a great addition and I truly hope this adds to the knowledge of the early days of Colorado.

Thank you, God, in heaven for the ability to work. With my brother, who had cerebral palsy, in mind, not everyone gets that gift. I am humbled to have the opportunity to work on compiling this small piece of history about those who came before us.

Introduction

As I worked on my "Old Boston: As Wild As They Come" I found myself enthralled with the news of yesteryear and with the frontier newspapermen of old. The more I read the news of yesteryear, the more I wanted to learn. I compiled numerous artifacts connected to Boston, Colorado which I didn't realize at the time was going to be the foundation for a series, consisting of the letters written by those coming west.

This compilation, *"When Colorado was still Kansas,"* is the latest compilation in my letters series. The year was 1859, it was a time before Colorado was known as Colorado. Denver, then known as Denver City was staked out in late 1858 in what was part of Kansas Territory. In fact, Denver and all of eastern Colorado was at the time a part of Kansas Territory.

There were residents of Denver pushing for the creation of Jefferson Territory in 1859, which Congress never recognized. The eastern part of Colorado remained a part of Kansas until 1861, when Colorado Territory was established. A complicated series of negotiations and compromises in the territory, and between it and Washington, resulted in the modern borders of Kansas and the creation of Colorado Territory. A matter of controversy, certainly, but by no means was this geographic consideration the most contentious in the region in the 1850s.

This compilation of letters, reports, and telegrams is from individuals and correspondents about places they came to visit and things they saw during this time. Although the focus is on the letters, I have added a few other newspaper artifacts such as advertisements and short news clipping to provide additional detail and context to era.

There are letters from people who had come west for their health, from those who were exploring and seeking their fortune and from those who were hiding from something in their past. These brave individuals; men, women, young and old; took to heart the phrase often attributed to Horace Greeley,

"Go west young man, go west and grow up with the country."

The letters compiled for this project tell of life in those days, sometimes good and sometimes not so good. In addition to the good news and the wonder people had about the American West, you will some-times find tragedy. I present content in the following order:

- Each chapter begins with one of my favorite quotes from that year.
- For each letter you will see:
  - The header for the message as they presented it in the old-time newspaper.

- o The paper in which they published the letter is listed, so you will know where the writer was from (There are exceptions).
- o The text from the letter. They often addressed it to the editor of the paper.
- o Commentary, if I have any or if it relates to a separate project. Sometimes I present foot-notes to support understanding of the content. I sometimes use footnotes to clarify abbreviations or locations.

There are also many alternate spellings and slang terms in old newspapers that may or may not have meaning. They also often spell canyon, "canon." The term cozy is spelled "cosy." Stayed is often spelled "staid." Rocky is often spelled "Rockie" or some other variation With this work you must assume that is the way they wrote it in the 1880s. Other things you will see include the use of the term Ultimo or ult. This refers to the previous month. A December newspaper which says "12th ult." is referring to November 12th. The term "&c." is often used in place of "etc." Understanding there are many variations of terms and abbreviations and spellings which are in error by modern standards. Understanding this will help with your enjoyment of this material. I hope you enjoy these letters as much as I have.

I have included letters that contain content which today may seem insensitive, biased, or culturally inappropriate. However, one aim of this project is to preserve the history and the perspective of what was occurring during that era so we can learn from it. There are parts of the past I wish we could see, but I am also thankful some things you will read have changed, and I am grateful for those who worked for such change.

These writings are part of the nostalgia of the old days and for which we sometimes long. Newspapers of the old days are a great way to learn more about those times. People were interested in the west as shown by the following excerpts,

The "Wheelbarrow Man," who passed through in September last, on his way to the gold mines, has landed at his point of destination, and written a long communication to the Pittsburgh *Post*, from which we clip the following: He writes from Denver City, at the mouth of Cherry Creek.

The *Kansas Tribune* (Lawrence, Kansas) 27 Jan 1859.

Often local newspapers were exchanged with other publications from places which settlers had moved. Those newspapers in the hometowns would then share with the community bits and pieces of the lives of former citizens. Those tidbits include reports of people traveling to engage in new vocations, marriage notices, deaths, and obits, murders, fights and shootings, legal notices, prices for commodities and more.

There was always some news sent home of interesting happenings in the area in which someone had previously resided. Letters sent "home" often explained with wonder a new place a person was visiting or was moving. Sending and receiving letters wasn't easy or cheap as the following excerpt indicates,

"I intended writing to the Times, but the mails are so uncertain — and besides it costs 50 to 60 cents to send a letter out and 55 cents to get one here."

For me there has been no better way to retrace the steps of those who traveled west in the 1800s. Through various letters written to the folks back home or to others for multiple purposes, political or otherwise we will look further into the soul of the early days of Colorado before it was Colorado.

Thanks for taking the time to read and I hope you enjoy reading this history as much as I have.

Chapter 1: 1859 January - March

"The health of the country is excellent, the air pure and bracing. In fact there is nothing out here to make it unhealthy except Taos (pronounced Touse) whiskey which is warranted to kill at 140 yards, or tan, a buffalo hide in fifteen minutes."

-Letter from Cherry Creek, 1859

Cherry Creek is in Kansas, about 40 miles south of the Nebraska line, and the mouth is 78 miles from Pike's Peak. Denver City, at the mouth of Cherry Creek, is the county seat of Arrapahoe county, which takes in the gold region, and was organized by an act of the Kansas Legislature two years ago. At the south of Cherry Creek the new town of Auraria is located, which bids far, it is claimed, to become the great city of the gold country. It is about the geographical centre as now discovered, and is surrounded by a good agricultural region. There are already 150 houses, or places where people live, in the city, and a paper to be called the Auraria Herald is to be started in the spring. Mr. Oscar B. Totten, well known in St. Louis, writes as follows from Denver City, Nov. 20th:

Cleveland Daily Leader (Cleveland, Ohio) 6 Jan 1859. — The gold is here, and men are now making from eight to twelve dollars per day, with pans and rockers; but the best prospects have been found in the mountains, and cannot be worked this winter, on account of the weather and water.

That this will prove a second California, have no doubt; and I think we will have a population of some 50,000 persons by next fall. All that are now here are satisfied with the prospects and the country. The farming land is good, rich in soil, and extends in the Platte and Cherry Creek valleys from 100 to 150 miles. There are also other creeks putting into the Platte, the valleys of which are equal to the Missouri river bottoms, well timbered and with plenty of good water. The officers appointed by Gov. Denver to organize a county, have selected this town for the county sent, which located at the junction of the Platte and Cherry Creek, and at the convergence of all the roads leading from the States and from Fort Union to Laramie, Salt Lake and Fort Bridger. There are now from 500 to 700 persons in the valley, all of whom are well pleased with the prospects, and think this the new Eldorado of the world.

> The "Wheelbarrow Man," who pass-
> ed through in September last, on his way
> to the gold mines, has landed at his point
> of destination, and written a long com-
> munication to the Pittsburgh *Post*, from
> which we clip the following: He writes
> from Denver City, at the mouth of Cher-
> ry Creek.

The *Kansas Tribune* (Lawrence, Kansas) 27 Jan 1859. — Reports reach us every day of the richness of the mines in other directions. Mr. Goodman, a mountaineer of twelve years standing, showed me some gold, last night, said to have been dug on the Cache le Poole, about thirty miles distant. It was of the kind known as "shot gold." He told me that miners were averaging $30 per day. It is also reported that a vein of most excellent coal, six feet in thickness, has been discovered not far from this place. I give these as reports and do not vouch for the truth of them. In fact, I shall vouch for the truth of nothing, except what I see. Every one here is in excellent spirits, and every one is alive with excitement. Farming claims are being taken up all around us, although the claimants will have to await a treaty with the Indians, and until the land is thrown into market before then-claims will be valid. Some of the claimants will marry Indian women and thus attempt to secure their claim. The Indians are very much dissatisfied at the whites passing through their county, and will in the

Spring send on a delegation to Washington, headed by the celebrated Kiawa Chief, Qhiamento, to demand remuneration for the whites passing thro' their lands. If they are successful, emigrants will have no difficulty, but if they are not, it will be dangerous for any but large parties, well-armed to come through.

Game of all kinds is plenty in the territory. We came up on our first buffalo at Cottonwood, and saw the last at the Arkansas crossing. The night after we left the big bend of the Arkansas a herd, numbering, as near as we could estimate, some 4,000 came upon our camp. We corelled our cattle as readily as possible, and then fired upon them. As they ran off they fairly shook the ground. In less than twenty minutes the wolves were on their track yelling and screaming frantically, showing that we had drawn blood. Prairie chickens, badgers, prairie dogs, antelopes, deer of every kind, prairie panthers, turkeys, geese, ducks, swans, bears both black and grizzly, and most every other species of game is in abundance. Two mountain goats were brought into town today. The health of the country is excellent, the air pure and bracing. In fact there is nothing out here to make it unhealthy except Taos (pronounced Touse) whiskey which is warranted to kill at 140 yards, or tan, a buffalo hide in fifteen minutes.

Altogether, a jollier crowd would be hard to find. Our old friend Gen. Larimer is in the tallest kind of spirits. The order of exercise is hard work all day and jollification at night. Although separated from home enjoyments and endearments, there is no repining; we take things as they come; and throw care to the dogs. As an occasional interlude, or grand *"pas de"* as many as can get in, the Indians give us their dances, commencing, with the scalp dance and going through their routine. We anticipate great things in the spring, and I only hope our anticipations will not be groundless. There is but one law recognized here at present, and the presiding Judge's name is Lynch. Rogues are honest by compulsion.

LETTER FROM CHERRY CREEK

Valuable Information!—A vast Field of Mineral Wealth !!—$5 to $15 per Day !!—Iron Ore discovered !—Splendid Agricultural Couutry !—Pine, Spruce, Oak & Cottonwood timber, —Directions to Emigrants !

The *Fort Scott Bulletin* (Fort Scott, Kansas) 27 Jan 1859. — A gentleman in this city has just received via Ft. Kearny, a private letter from a friend in the mines, whose statements can be relied upon in every particular and who represents that his most sanguine expectations have been more than realized. The country is rich in mineral wealth, and is as fine an agricultural region as any portion of Kansas. We make the following extract from his letter, which is dated Cherry Creek; Nov. 20th, 1858.

You need no longer doubt about the gold in this region. It is a fixed fact. Every portion of the country is teeming, with mineral wealth. The miners are making from $5 to 15 per day, with the rudest of implements, and with no facilities for mining greater than picks and pans, and long toms. I have prospected a large scope of country, and speak from personal knowledge, when I say that fortunes can and will be made here. You can depend upon this. Advise all who think of coming out, to start a six months supply of provisions and to come in companies if possible. They will get along much better and can assist each other in case of emergency.

The country is as fine an agricultural one as you will find anywhere in the eastern portion of Kansas, and the timber is a Pine, Spruce, Oak, and abound. Specimens or iron have been found by many persons, but the miners are after a richer metal, and pay no attention to it.

"Be sure and bring along plenty of the same. Provisions are very high now and will be much higher. Everything is prospering. Several new towns have been laid out, and the cabins of the miners are springing up in every direction. Companies are still arriving and I think over 1000 people are already here. I believe we will have 20,000 people here by next winter. All now here are satisfied with the prospects, and everybody thinks the mines are as rich as those of California."

From the Leavenworth Times.

LETTER FROM A MAN WHO

MADE NEARLY A THOUSAND A WEEK.— General Eastin has handed us the following letter, for the reliability of which he stands responsible. If true, it makes the Gold District a perfect bed of gold. We give the letter without further comments :

December 20, 1859.

DEAR GENERAL : I arrived at Leavenworth City yesterday, and as everybody is contributing to your paper something from Cherry Creek gold diggings, I thought I would tell you what I did while I was there.

I arrived on the 20th of August, and prospected through the country for some time, and at last struck a vein about twenty-nine and a half miles south of Cherry Creek that in richness exceeded anything that had been discovered. I dug out of this vein, in twenty-five days $3,000 worth of gold, and the vein did not seem to be exhausted in any degree.

Yours truly, JOHN HARTMAN.

The *Fort Scott Bulletin* (Fort Scott, Kansas) 27 Jan 1859.

☞ Gen. Larimer writes from the Pike Peak region, to the Leavenworth *Times*, and sends some gold dust. Gen. L., who dates from Denver City, says, "we have good reports every day from the mines, about 8 miles from here. The miners, are taking out from twenty-five to fifty cents per pan."

It is a remarkable fact that the rich gold digings are always a *little way* off. Never right there, but like an *ignis fatuus*, plainly in sight but never within reach. The tide of gold seekers that will flow West on the opening of Spring will have had no parallel in this land, and disappointment, disease, suffering and death will follow. The most tremendous efforts are being made. by interested parties, through the medium of the press to encourage this emigration, and the number of young men who will give up comfortable homes, and sacrifice reasonable prospects, in chase of gold veins will be legion.

The *Holmes County Republican* (Millersburg, Ohio) 10 Feb 1859.

As was seen in yesterday's Gazette, the House of Representatives has laid on the table—killed, for the present—the bills establishing territorial governments in Arizona, Dacotah, and Jefferson territories. The Washington correspondent of the Baltimore Sun says:—"A number of circumstances concur, at present, to prevent the passage of these bills. Any increase of executive patronage or expenditure is much deprecated, and, besides, the southern members think that free States are growing up in the West fast enough, without the application of any forcing legislation."

Alexandria Gazette (Alexandria, Virginia) 18 Feb 1859.

FROM THE GOLD MINES!

THE VERY LATEST NEWS FROM CHERRY CREEK!

ALL PREVIOUS ACCOUNTS CONFIRMED!

GLOWING ACCOUNTS.

The North Platte Route the Best!!

ROUND GOLD FOUND.

Extracts from Interesting Letters from Reliable Sources.

Gold! Gold! Gold!

[From the Omaha (Nebraska) Times.]

The *States and Union* (Ashland, Ohio) 23 Feb 1859. — Company arrived in our city on last Tuesday, direct from the Cherry Creek gold mines, but as they immediately passed over to Iowa, we were unable to procure any concise statement from them, but enough to get the general import of the news in the Mining Region. — They bring the most glowing accounts yet received. The news seems like the glad shouts of triumph which makes the heavens ring with very joy when the victory is won, doubt is removed. We append some letters written by known to be reliable. The first is from Edward Mather, formerly county clerk of Washington County, and with whom nearly all our citizens have a personal acquaintance and for whom all his acquaintances stand ready to vouch. We have only space to give extracts. He writes from Denver City:

"There have been some new discoveries since I wrote you last; still not much mining has been done. "One company, who have been working during the past few days, have done splendidly, averaging **EIGHT DOLLARS A DAY** to the man; they only worked five hours per day for this. The general average with parties has been from three to "four dollars; but men who have prospected the country thoroughly, insist that they can make **TWENTY DOLLARS PER DAY** with, long toms."

There are many rumors, but I only desire to communicate facts to you. A party of men from Nebraska City are now prospecting in the mountains; they have found "shot gold," but how they are getting along, or what wages they are making, we have, not yet heard anything upon which we can rely.

Write to our friends in Wisconsin and Illinois to come out, and to be sure to take the North Platte Valley Route. Our companies always beat those from Leavenworth and Kansas City by at least twelve or fifteen days. Do our readers want anything more positive or conclusive than this, either upon the route or the mines? Note how careful he is not to abuse the confidence of, his friends, by giving credit to flying rumors — how particular to give the facts without coloring, and yet how positive in his statements relative to the mines and the route. Of life in the mines, Philip Scheever says:

"We spend our evenings very socially. We sometimes read, and quite as often play at cards. We are saving a quart of whisky and a box of sardines for the holidays, when we expect to have a grand jollification." And Andrew Sagendorf, on the same subject, says:

"There are charms about this country; the scenery, the climate, and the excitement of the chase, are alone enough to overcome all longings after home, and the thousand and one little joys and comforts of an Eastern life. Here, every night an enchanting dream. Wrapped in a blanket, with mother earth for a pillow, and the starry heavens for a roof, the sleeper in his dreams lives over the pet joys of days long past."

He also says:

"We made better time with our ox teams, and so did the Council Bluffs boys, than any parties that came by the South Platte-route. — If you come out, be sure, to take the North Platte route."

"Shot gold has been discovered in two canons, through which Cache La Poode and Thompson's Creek make their way out of the mountains."

"I looked upon the first specimen of Quartz Gold that has been found. It came from the canon of Thompson's Fork, and is quite rich."

Henry Allen, lately a member of the Iowa Legislature, and Postmaster at Council Bluffs, a gentleman of known integrity and extensive acquaintance, writes a very interesting letter to his wife, which we find in yesterday's *Bugle*, and from which we make a few extracts.

His statements, at all times and under all circumstances reliable, are rendered doubly so in this instance, when writing to his wife and daughters, whom he would not deceive. Read what he says:

"I have panned out forty-five cents worth in one pan full of dirt. It is very fine. I think with the right kind of tools, a person can make from five to twenty dollars per day."

"In this letter, I send you seventy-five cents worth of gold. This I got out of two pans of dirt."

"I know where there are diggings in which the gold is larger than this. I have seen some about the size of a common white bean; but it is impossible to do anything like work in the winter, but when spring opens we will be in, certain."

"You will doubtless see persons who have returned from here, dissatisfied with the country and everything out here; but such persons would not be satisfied in any place. This, I can assure my friends, that any man that will work will make money. All that is wanted is industry to insure a fortune here."

"Old Californians have no advantage over the rest of us, from the fact that the diggings here beats them out — they are not confined to any locality; but are scattered over the whole country for a distance of over two hundred miles. The whole country appears to be impregnated with gold."

William Clancy, formerly a prominent man in this Territory, writes:

"Gold exists over a space of country extending from the Arkansas in the South, to the Medicine Bow river in the North. There is abundance of pine and cottonwood timber here."

Gen. Larimer, formerly a banker in Pittsburgh, and a prominent man in Western Pennsylvania, and more recently of this Territory writing to his friends from his new home in the Nebraska mines, says:

"Miners are making from three to five dollars per day, with good prospects of doing better in the Spring."

We could keep on to any length but don't think it necessary, and will therefore conclude with an extract from a letter to Samuel Curtis to the *Nonpariel*. Curtis is a son of the Iowa Congressman of that name who introduced the Pacific Railroad Bill, and when he writes, he writes the truth. Here are the extracts:

"There has been but little done as yet in the mines. A company has been formed to dig a ditch, for the purpose of turning the waters of a small stream near here. The banks of the stream pay, for half a mile back, and for seven miles in length, from five to thirty-five cents to the pan, from the surface down to the bed rock. All the gold that has been found is float gold. Reports are in circulation of the discovery of both shot, or lump gold, and gold quartz. I have seen none of either, although I think it is here. Those who have been here all summer are not experienced miners, and may not have found it, if they have, they do not tell where it is. All the old miners with whom I have talked, are satisfied that there is gold here in sufficient quantities to pay for mining. Yesterday, the 26th, a train came in from Sioux

City, Smithland and that vicinity, and they are all in good health and spirits. They report that the excitement is still on the increase in the States. I think that all reasonable reports that you hear at present, will be more than realized next summer."

ANOTHER LETTER FROM MR. WARREN.

Additional Particulars — Fuller Accounts about the Gold and Country Prices of Provisions, Clothing, Lumber, &c, &c,

Through the kindness of Mr. Thomas West, we are enabled to lay before our readers this morning, another letter from Mr. Thos. Warren, whose communications appear to contain more interesting and useful matter, than any other letters that have as yet been published — *Kansas City Journal.*

MONTANA, Dec. 11, 1858.

THOS. WEST; Esq., Kansas City:

Dear Sir: Since my last letter to you, I have arrived herein the heart of the gold region, and am now able to give you my own impressions. I am snugly cabined for the winter, and with the exception of a frozen foot, am as comfortable as heart could wish.

My anticipations in regard to this country have been more than realized, and although the weather has been of such a nature as to preclude the possibility of mining to any great extent, still I have seen enough to justify me in believing that gold exists in great abundance, and that the opening of spring will disclose its rich treasure to us. It is almost impossible to find a discontented, dissatisfied, or disappointed man in the country. All are sanguine, and the expression's of opinion of old California miners, that the prospects of a rich golden harvest is not excelled even by the mines of California, causes us all to look forward with joyful anticipations to the future.

My last was written under the disadvantageous circumstances of no pen and ink, and on the open prairie with the wind blowing a gale. Not while surrounded at least with some of the comforts of life, I shall endeavor to supply the deficiencies that occurred in that letter.

In this part of the country, then, are some good farming lands along the valley of Cherry Creek, Platte river, and towards the mountains. Two flourishing towns are laid off five miles below this, at the mouth of Cherry Creek, one called Auraria, signifying Golden Light, and the other Denver City. Two and a half miles above this place, is another town known as Nonpareil City, so that you see we are well supplied with towns. One word how in regard to supplies and wants, and then for the mines. Provisions are scarce, and prices are exorbitant. Flour is worth $30 per cwt., and Mexican flour is worth $20 to $25 per "finagre," or Mexican measure of 145 pounds. - Beans are worth $15 per bushel, coffee 50 cents, salt 25 cents, sugar 50 cts., bacon 50 cents, and very-scarce, beef 15 cents, butter $1.25, venison 5, and other things in proportion. Whisky is worth $16 per gallon, and Taos or Mexican whisky, $8. Clothing is not in the market, with the exception of undershirts, drawers and socks. Game of all kinds exists in the greatest abundance, and many are having clothes-made out of the skins of wild animals. A large number of the population have been and still are engaged in hunting, and wagons are daily returning from the mountains loaded with game. And now for the mines. As yet, but few have been engaged in mining, and those who have worked their claims, have worked but very little, and that, too, with very inferior implements, pans being the principal thing used, although some, half dozen have rockers dug out of cotton wood trees. They have made from $1 to $10 per day. This is winter work, with every disadvantage on their side. New mines have been discovered at Table Mountain, some twelve miles from this, the dirt of which, it is said, pays fifty cents to the pan. A great many have gone over there to take up claims for the spring. The Cache le Pool mines, thirty miles North of this, it is said, are paying very largely. The gold from the latter mines is what is known as "shot gold." The Dry Creek mines are inciting considerable attention, and nearly all the claims are taken along that stream. The gold appears to be very equally distributed all over the country, and it is impossible to dig to the bed rock anywhere without finding the color. The Georgia Company acknowledge that they know of diggings that are far superior to any I have mentioned, but refuse to make known their locality until spring.

The name "Pike's Peak" gold mines, is an improper one, and originated from the fact that the Lawrence company of prospectors were dancing around Pike's Peak last summer, when the excitement broke out. They should be called the South Platte mines. Pike's Peak about eighty miles south of us, and Long's Peak is to the north of us, and from here is a much more prominent land mark. Over what an extent of country the mines reach, it is impossible as yet to conjecture, for the prospecting in the South Park, and on the South waters, is as rich as it is here, but the jealousy of the Utah Indians, has thus far prevented prospecting in that direction to any great extent. All the other tribes in this section are on good terms with us, visiting us freely, and trading their peltry for anything we have to spare. I suppose I do not exaggerate when I say that at least five hundred buildings are now in progress of erection in Denver City and Auraria, in anticipation of a general rush in the spring. A saw-mill is much needed here, and would prove a rich speculation to the proprietor. Inferior lumber, ripped out with a whip saw is worth $25 per 100 feet at present. A very large ice house is being built here, and our folks will have something to cool them during the heat of summer. To all who propose coming out here in the spring, I would advise them to bring a supply of good clothing and plenty of provisions, also tools, whether they are mechanics or not.

In case that any new discoveries are made, I advise you of the fact. If you could send me a few papers they would be a rich treat to us poor isolated mortals.

Yours, **THOS. WARREN.**

THURSDAY MORNING, FEB. 24.

Pike's Peak.

From all parts of the State our exchanges bring us word that companies are starting, or getting ready to start, for the land of gold. Hardly a paper but what has something to say in relation to the propriety of going. We have no counsel to offer upon the subject, but subjoin the latest reliable advices. A letter from Mr. P. T. BASSETT, formerly of St. Louis, dated at Denver City, mouth of Cherry Creek, 75 or 80 miles north of Pike's Peak, January 1st, furnishes the following:

Alton Weekly Telegraph (Alton, Illinois) 24 Feb 1859. — "I can assure you that what you read is no exaggeration, for it is what I see myself. What I have done I will tell you. I have some days taken out myself from $5 to $10 with a rocker; but it is hard work, for there is not water to work with. In the spring I hope to do better than now. This is about the average of the mines, or the lack of water. There is not more than 1/3; the rest are building houses in the different towns that have been laid out here."

"There are about 2,000 persons in this Valley, and arriving every day. I hear that many are detained at the Crossing of the South

Platte, on account of the snow, and that the snow is very deep in that direction. This I learned by the Indians. Provisions are very high and scarce. Flour $15 per sack; sugar 50 cents per pound; coffee 50 cents per pound, and everything else in proportion.

"I suppose you want to know what the prospects are for trading. I cannot advise you, for I think that everybody has written home to their friends to come and bring something to sell. You can judge for yourself how much and how many goods will come from the States, and then add to this amount one-third from New Mexico."

> Another letter, of same date and from same place, written by Mr. R. Cockright, lately of Dixon, Ills., known to one of the employees of this office as a young man whose statements can be relied upon to the fullest extent, furnishes these extracts :

Alton Weekly Telegraph (Alton, Illinois) 24 Feb 1859. —"We have had very pleasant weather here so far— finest I ever saw. We can see the snow-capped mountains in snowfall in every day, and yet in the village where we are it apears like spring. We are so near the mountains do we have no winds. The air is pure in the warm sun shines down upon us at midday as if it were July.

"I cannot give you much news about the mine, as the weather has been rather too cold to work in the water; but it is my impression that will be good wages made here next Spring and Summer — There, of course, a great many come here next spring they're not willing to work, and expect to make a fortune in a few days. Men can do far better here in the spring than they can in the states; at least that is my opinion."

MR. COURTWRIGHT, Writing to his Dixon friends, advises them not to outfit till they get to the Western border of Iowa.

A third letter, written from Pike's Peak City, on the 4th of January, says:

Alton Weekly Telegraph (**Alton, Illinois) 24 Feb 1859.** — "The miners are mostly prospecting for spring digging, and most of them, that is of the working class are doing well, I mean well for the winter, considering the inferior way in which they have to mine— with pans mostly— As the frozen ground will not admit a very expensive working. When I say the miners are doing well, I mean they are making over $5 per day; for if a minor starts out prospecting, and cannot average $5 per day, he says he has done nothing. But the largest strike that has been made by one man in this part of the mines was $75 in one day, with the pick and a pan. The lucky man was Mr. J.W. Stanley, from Mineral Point Wisconsin— the largest nugget that I have seen, Wayne just $11 10,[4] but the golden is part of the country's very fine scale gold.

The Indians are very friendly so far— provisions are getting rather scarce and command a good price. Flour 30 cents per pound, bacon 25, coffee 30, sugar 30, beans 20, rice 30, dried apples, 50 tobacco $1.75, whisky $18.00 per gallon, with $2.50 worth of tobacco and strychnine in each gallon."

> A particularly intelligent and moderate-toned letter from Denver City, January 15th, after reiterating that the climate is the finest in the world, almost, and that the weather is delightful continues:

Alton Weekly Telegraph (**Alton, Illinois**) **24 Feb 1859.** — "If anyone will come out here, I can take him to a spot where he and I can dig and work out $2 at $3 each per day, with a pan, and at the same time discuss all the political topics of the day; and if one strong-armed young, experienced miner will go to work as though he was in earnest, he can dig out his $5 or $8 per day with the full hope of a grand strike every hour. The fact is, we have had no time to prospect or dig, nor will we have until spring, and then you may expect to hear the richest kind of digging with long tongues and sluices. Besides quartz has been discovered bearing gold."

The writer remarks that they have preaching at Denver City every other Sunday; but the people have supplies enough to last till the first and middle of May; that claims are being taken all over the country, more particularly in the choicest spots on Cherry Creek, and up and down the South Platte; that Denver city has now over one hundred houses built and underway, comprising "fair-size" hotels in 64 by 96 feet which is intended for a public hall. In regard to the want of the country he observes,

"We need many things here, such as sawmills, glass, nails and all kinds of finishing materials of the cheapest kind. We have now beautiful Pine Lumber at 20 cents per foot, cut with whipsaw; also Cottonwood boards cut in the same way. We also need many things that the immigrant could just as well bring as not. Wagon to bring a nice coop of fowls; also small pigs. Milch cows could easily work as oxen — at least one pair for each wagon. We need these things very much. I only know of two milch cows in the country, with one lot of fowls and pigs. Bacon is also wanted, or lard. Cows, dogs, and fouls, would add much to our table comfort. We have a fair supply of Mexican potatoes at $5 per bushel, Mexican flour at $15 per hundred pounds; what every immigrant should bring flour, as I have no idea that New Mexico can supply us, they having only three regular meals in the whole territory."

Further From Pike's Peak.

From a letter written at Auraria City, mouth of Cherry Creek, on the 6th of January, by gentlemen from St. Louis, we extract as follows in relation to the gold prospects. The italics are ours.

Alton Weekly Telegraph (Alton, Illinois) · 24 Feb 1859. — "There's plenty of gold here, or in the vicinity, but it is scattered over a large surface of country, and is very fine. Few men are mining now, but are making from $3 to $5 and $8 per day. We would not advise anyone who is doing well in the state to come out here, but in all that are situated like we were I would say come. So, Mr. Smith, tell all of your friends at the house when you receive this, that this is a fine country, and there will be a large quantity of gold dug here next summer, and they may get a portion of it. It is the opinion of all here that there are large deposits in this country. I can take a pick and go out here anywhere, and find gold, but it will not pay to work at. It only pays along the watercourses. We are in hopes to give you a better account the next time we write, and the weather has been most cold to prospect much."

The same letter says the land is good for farming; that the weather, the cold on the mountains, is very pleasant; at the South

Platte and its tributaries are heavily timbered, and the mountains covered with pines; that there is a great abundance of game, such as Elk, Mountain sheep, antelope &c.; that the Indians yet are very friendly.

A letter received from the same City by a gentleman in the St. Louis *News* office, dated on the 20th inst. which we believe is the latest date yet from the gold region, says (and the italics in this case are also our own);

Alton Weekly Telegraph (Alton, Illinois) 24 Feb 1859. — Everyday brings additional discoveries of gold and it is now found in every direction around us. A few days ago, I witnessed some men working up the Platte, but two miles from here. I took from a hole some dirt and paint it and got about $0.08. They told me they were making about $6 per day, although they had to carry their dirt about 200 yards to water and it was so cold I could not half work with a rocker. I can safely say to you and my friends that a man provided with good tools, and good weather, can make $5 a day. The diggers do not work now more than about 4 hours of the day, at noon when it is warm. I am prospecting and have not yet found anything more than I have mentioned. I would advise those at home who are doing well to stay where they are; but if there are any young men who were fond of hard work and want to try their luck— let them come along.— They can make something, and learn a great deal. Those who come I would advise him to come up to Platte, as it is the best road and much the shortest route. Packing out as preferable, this person can make this trip in 20 days.

A Mr. H. L. Bolton, formerly of St. Louis, several of whose published letters have come under our observation, and who seems to be a very intelligent and sensible writer, from Auraria City, under date of January 19th, thus speaks, after confirming all other accounts in relation to the agreeableness of the climate, and the openness of the winter:

Alton Weekly Telegraph (Alton, Illinois) · **24 Feb 1859.** — "Some persons have already commenced to working in the mines; so far pays poorly. Diggers who have been most successful have not average $3 per day, and some have not made 50 cents, working hard at that. The gold is very fine. It takes from 25 particles to make the value of a cent. The largest spec which I have heard of, will not weigh more than $0.25 in value. All the large lumps that you have received in St Louis, as Pikes Peak gold were never obtained in this region — they belong to California. All the accounts of gold findings of an extravagant character, are the fabrication to speculators. I wish to put you and others on their guard against these stories; especially General Larimer account. I will venture to say that he does not know anything about the matter. How to influence the outcome of the election I offend a good prospect yet; and I am on the ground. I've ventured a prediction that few persons will make fortunes and some find gold in this country. But is "seeing is believing" that all those who wish to have a sight at the "elephant" come on. I am beginning to get a view of him.

There are more the 200 cabins built here; and two hundred more to be erected before the last of March. A good hotel will be ready for" the boarders" by the end of May. It is to be two stories high, 75 feet in width, and 120 feet in length. Speculators are already busily engaged and laying off cities, around the diggings, and there are fellows sending to the states such glowing account of gold discoveries.

If enough of gold is not found before the latter part of May, many now here we'll go to California, New Mexico and Arizona, while not a few will pitch their tents in this new region for life?

Those who contemplate going to this new Eldorado must draw their own conclusions. It will be observed; the tone of these letters is quite different from that of those published yesterday. The letter of Mr. Bolton concludes by saying: "The principal amusement here during the winter has been card playing, telling yarns, and drinking the most excusable whiskey. The latter is worth $10 per gallon — in St

Louis it would cost 20 cents. I must not have meant to tell you that I have not seen a white woman since I left the states."

A letter from Cherry Creek, says that no gold dust has been sold there for less than $20 per ounce.

The *Weekly News-Democrat* (Emporia, Kansas) 19 Mar 1859.

"There is gold here — lots of it. The gophers dig it out of the ground by the bushel, and in the moonlight the whole earth for miles around looks like heaven with its myriad stars, or like a pretty girl with yellow freckles."

-Letter from Colorado, 1859

The people of Upper Mexico are desirous of annexation to Jefferson territory.

The Tennessean (Nashville, Tennessee) 3 Apr 1859.

[From the Milwaukee News.]
Letter from Pikes Peak.
We give below a letter written from Pike's Peak, by a well known citizen of Horicon, now at Pike's Peak. Every word can be relied upon as true, as the writer is well known in Wisconsin as a man who has the greatest regard for the truth. There is evidently gold there.
PIKE'S PEAK, March 1, 1859.

The *Daily Empire* (Dayton, Ohio) 21 Apr 1859. — DEAR BROTHER: I promise to write you a long letter as soon as I arrived here, and I take my pen in hand to let you know that we are all well, it's a hope these few lines will find you enjoying the same blessing. You know we left Horicon for the land of gold about the 1st of February, and we arrived here yesterday. My wife did the journey first-rate, but my five oldest boys were nearly tired out when they reached here. Jane, the little sis is happy as a lark, and says "tiss Uncle George for me."

God bless her sweet heart. We had all the hardships in the world before we got here. We lost our horses at Dubuque — They were stolen from us. We got some oxen, and lost them 100 miles from Omaha. Then we tried wheelbarrows, my wife and I wheeling by turns, till the Indians stole are barrows. We then walked, till the Indians stole our provisions, and my family got sick, so I had to carry them all on my back. Our money gave out long before, and for two weeks we travel through a wilderness where the foot of a human being had never trod, in this condition, seeing no living being, and without money to purchase even a cracker at any of the groceries along the line. We lived on roots till my children all looked like pigs, from rooting as long, and I've carried my family on my back that I am so round shoulder that I can see the blue sky and the bright sun, by looking between my legs and up to Heaven's panoply that way. I lost two hundred pounds of flesh — horse meat — when I started from Dubuque or we should have got along better.

I read in the Milwaukee news Pike's Peak was a humbug, but it ain't, and the news knows as well as I do. We got here in the morning, after walking all night, and though we are now 24 hours in the country, are not well off, but have a good prospect.

There is gold here — lots of it. The gophers dig it out of the ground by the bushel, and in the moonlight the whole earth for miles around looks like heaven with its myriad stars, or like a pretty girl with yellow freckles. The woodchucks dig out bushels and bushels of it, and the snakes in this country look like solid gold ones, from crawling among the gold chunks. It is found in all size pieces, from the size of a hen's egg up to the bigness of a large stone, and of the finest quality. We have raked together what lay loose on an acre of ground, and have a twenty two piles about as big as large size haystack. Last night two hundred Indians came to rob us of a set of silver spoons in a fine comb that my wife had to use on the children, and we barricaded our house with rocks of gold till they could not gain admittance and were forced to beg to make friends with us. The chief lay down his weapons in came into our camp when my wife used the fine comb on his head till his gratitude was as lively as his head was, and he was so tickled that he offered to marry my wife and show me where gold was in plenty. I love my wife, you know that George, the thinking that I might die before I got rich, and feeling I must make some property to leave my children, I consented to the match, and she has gone off with the Indian, who is a great chief, and taking the fine comb with her. Come out with your wife, and bring a fine comb brother George.

I'm going to leave these diggings for a better one. It is too much trouble to tug and pry big chunks of gold that weigh a half a ton or so, and are so thick you cannot get them out without danger of breaking your legs, and I am going up to a ravine, where all I have to do is to go to the top of a high mountain and roll it down to the river.

The country here is fine, but the winds are awful. My boys got so light with eating roots, that I can only keep them with me, or together by piling lumps of gold, about as big as mallets, on their shirt tails, as the little innocents sit down on the grass to play. Everything is grown here. I can raise twenty bushels of wheat to the acre. Oranges, lemons and all such colored fruits grow wild here. While melons, pears, apples, peaches, apple dumplings, are so plenty but they find no market.

Sell off what stuff you have in Wisconsin, and come out here. You can get rich in a little while, and go back and such style that it will astonish the natives.

Give my love to all the folks around the corners, and put a notice on the schoolhouse that they can get an outfit in Chicago for $200. Come out here dear brother by all means. Yours, affectionately,[5]

JOHN SMITH.

The Rock Island Argus has the following in a late letter from the Pike's Peak gold mines :—

"In Arrapahoe county there are from eight to twelve hundred poor devils, like myself, hunting gold, but not finding any. At present we are preparing to skin the spring emigration, which is to be done by disposing of town sites and bad whiskey."

North Star (Danville, Vermont) 23 Apr 1859.

Lynch Law at the Pike's Peak Gold Mines
Full Particulars.

A letter from Denver city, under date of April 8th, furnishes the following particulars of a case of Lynch law, already alluded to by the telegraph :

The *Hillsdale Standard* (Hillsdale, Michigan) 17 May 1859. —"I stated above that this has been a day of uncommon excitement. So it has, and a solemn day, Judge Lynch, today, hung a man for murder, and as the corpse of the murderer lay side-by-side with that of the victim, no one could feel that the act justified the result. The particulars are as follows: some three months since a party consisting of one old man by the name of Reingraff, in company with his sons. — Antonie and Phillip, son in law, John Stuffle, and John Ellis, all Germans, arrived here from Louisville Ky. Yesterday the body of Beingraff was discovered on Clear Creek about 7 miles from this place — his corpse was brought to town, and examination evidence was brought to light pretended to throw suspicion upon the son-in-law John Stuffle parties were sent in pursuit of him, who captured him about daylight this morning as he was returning to his home. He was brought to town and Court convened, Judge Smith presiding. The jury was composed of 12 of the most respectable persons in our community, was selected, and the prisoner given a fair trial. The jury, after an hour's deliberation returned a verdict of wilful murder. He was committed, without bail to stand his trial at the next term of the Criminal Court and the prisoner was remanded to the custody of the sheriff.

One of the officers of Judge Lynch Court then moved that the prisoner be allowed one half hours time to prepare for eternity. He was allowed a spiritual advisor (Rev. Mr. Fisher.) and at the expiration of three quarters of an hour was led to the place of execution. The rope has been thrown over a limb of a tree and a wagon placed under it. The prisoner came very composedly forward, mounted the wagon and made a speech, which blasphemy and raving took a prominent part. The wagon was drawn from under him during his struggle. The old man is also missing and it is supposed to be a meditated plot between the son Philipp and son-in-law to get the old man and Antonie out of the way, and then take the property, as Antoine's body was robbed when found— Both of the other Germans are now in custody, and it is thought that the brother will swing tomorrow. Gen Larimer conducted the defense and Henry Allen, Esq. the prosecution.

Capt. Preston, who went ahead as an avant courier of Russel & Jones' Express arrived yesterday and returns tomorrow. — His mission was to select the shortest route and arrange stations for the ensuing season. Capt. Wm. Smith also arrived to day just as the execution took place.   As time and opportunity allow I will endeavor to keep you somewhat posted in regard to matters in this neck of timber.

Ever yours,   A. C. SMITH.

THE KANSAS MINES.—In the Davenport Democrat we find a letter from Nebraska city of the 28th of April, from which we extract the following :

In the wake of the favorable intelligence which I have heretofore reported now comes news of a most discouraging character. Two men, Messrs. McCandlass and Travioh, of Taylor county, Iowa, who left this city some five weeks since, returned last evening, having proceeded only as far as Fort Kearny. They state that the Fort and the immediate vicinity is filled with persons who have returned from the mines and are begging their way home from emigrants. These returned miners state that the " gold in the mountains," regarding which so many expectations have been indulged, is a total failure, and that the Cherry Creek gold mines are a most unmitigated humbug. The two men of whom I have spoken, also state that on the day before they left Fort Kearny, Major Morris, the commander at that station, received a letter from Cherry Creek, to the effect that two men who had been prominent as letter writers during the winter, had been hung by a party of exasperated emigrants whom they had humbugged. They represent that there has been an immense amount of suffering upon the road, and that in instances, persons who have started out poor for the mines, have perished from cold, and in some cases, from actual starvation.

These statements I give you for what they are worth, it being impossible, from the contradictory character of the advices, for me to determine any thing regarding the matter. The persons who brought the intelligence appeared to be fair and candid men, and their statements have created quite an impression among the many emigrants who are camped in town. We shall not, of course, turn back unless something certain is obtained.

The *New Orleans Crescent* (New Orleans, Louisiana) 17 May 1859

DISTRESS AT PIKE'S PEAK.—A letter from Nebraska City gives dismal accounts obtained from men returning from Fort Kearney, who had made up their minds that it was not worth while to go on :

"They state that the Fort and the immediate vicinity is filled with persons who have returned from the mines and are begging their way home from emigrants. These returned miners state that the 'gold in the mountains,' regarding which so many expectations have been indulged, is a total failure and that the Cherry Creek gold mines are a most unmitigated humbug. On the day before they left Fort Kearney, Maj. Morris the commander at that station, received a letter from Cherry Creek, to the effect that two men who had been prominent as letter-writers during the winter had been hung by a party of exasperated emigrants whom they had humbugged. They represent that there has been an immense amount of suffering upon the road, and that in instances persons who have started out poor for the mines have perished from cold, and in some cases of actual starvation."

Vermont Standard (Woodstock, Vermont) 20 May 1859.

From Denver City—The Pike's Peak Gold Mines.

LEAVENWORTH, May 20.—The first overland express from Denver City arrived here this morning, having been ten days on the way. Four passengers and $700 in shot and scale gold came with the express. The advices from Denver city state that on the 8th a large force was employed in building ditches along Cherry Creek. The accounts from the mountains conflict. There was still too much snow and ice to operate with advantage. The general aspect of the news is favorable. The dust received is valued at $20 per ounce.

The *Daily Exchange (*Baltimore, Maryland) 21 May 1859.

FROM PIKE'S PEAK.

New England Farmer (Boston, Massachusetts) · 21 May 1859. —

A Letter from Denver city state that there is a great scarcity of provisions in the mines at Pike's Peak, and much suffering among the emigrants. Several deaths were reported from starvation, and the emigrants were in a destitute condition. An abundance of provisions is, however, on the way from here and other points. Contradictory reports prevailed regarding mining prospects. The general tenor of the intelligence, however, is not encouraging, but the unfavorable accounts are ascribed to the destitution and discontented emigrants. No remittances of dust or rich discoveries are announced. Measures have been initiated for a new State. Delegates are to meet at Denver City in June to form a State Constitution.

A letter dated Fort Kearney, 8th inst, says the Pike's Peak emigrants are returning in droves. Nine hundred wagons had passed the Fort in a week. The emigrants were in an extremely destitute condition, and selling their wagons, horses and outfits for almost nothing. The St. Joseph's Gazette publishes a report of a serious difficulty between the inhabitants of Auroria and Denver City, resulting in the burning of both towns. Local rivalry was said to be the cause. The report needs confirmation. The St Joseph correspondent of the Democrat notices the arrival at that place of one hundred Pike Peakers, who give deplorable accounts of mining prospects, and the suffering on the Plains. It is estimated that 30,000 men are on their way thither, all or most of whom are destitute of money and the necessaries of life, and perfectly reckless. Desperate threats are made of burning Omaha, St. Josephs, Leavenworth and other towns, in consequence of the deceptions used to induce emigration. Two thousand men are reported fifty miles west of Omaha, in a starving condition. Some of the residents of Plattsmouth have closed up their business and fled, fearing violence at the hands of the enraged emigrants.

A correspondent of the St. Joseph (Mo.) *Journal*, writing from Fort Kearney, Kansas, under date of the 8th inst., says:

Knowing that you take an interest in all things appertaining to the gold mines, I will let you know how the Pike's Peakers get along out here. They are all returning and not less 900 wagons passed here within the last week. They are selling their outfits for almost a song out here. They sell their flour from three to five dollars; bacon at ten cents; horses and cattle are selling for almost nothing, and wagons and handcarts they give away. There are some returning who have not one cent to take them back, while those who have any are hurrying home as fast as they can to keep from being robbed by the rest.

Now, sir, I am not interested in any way in this humbug as they call it, but I pity them if they are fooled, for ther eare a great many good and useful men who would do better at home with their families. On the other hand there are a great many scoundrels and good-for nothing rowdies out here, which will be a great good to the States if they never return again.

Nashville Union and American

(Nashville, Tennessee) 22 May 1859.

The unfavorable reports lately received from Pike's Peak have caused a general panic among the outward-bound emigrants, who are returning in large numbers. Meanwhile the latest intelligence from the mines is more favorable than ever. The majority of the returning emigrants have only been as far as Ft. Kearny. It is impossible to reconcile the conflicting statements, and the arrival of the expected shipments of dust is necessary to restore confidence in the practicability of the mines.

LATER.—The first overland express direct from Denver City, arrived here this morning. Ten days only were occupied in making the trip. Four passengers came through. The stage also brought $700 in gold dust, both scale and shot.

Advices to the 9th from Denver City, report a large force employed in building ditches along Cherry Creek. One long tom with a limited supply of water yielded an ounce the first day.

Accounts from the mountains were conflicting; some encouraging and others the reverse.

There was still too much snow and ice to operate to any advantage. The general aspect of the news is favorable. Gold will continue to arrive by the succeeding stages. The miners hold it at $20 per ounce.

The route which is 625 miles in length is pronounced to possess superior facilities, as is evidenced by the quickness of this the first trip.

The *Pantagraph* (Bloomington, Illinois) 23 May 1859.

Cleveland Daily Leader (**Cleveland, Ohio**) **28 May 1859.** —The accounts from Pikes Peak and vicinity are conflicting as ever, many of the returning miners pronouncing the whole thing a humbug of the first water, and others all there "fancy painted it." Two newspapers, the *Cherry Creek Pioneer* and the *Rocky Mountain News*, have been established, and both speak in flattering terms of the gold prospect. The news states that large forces are at work on the Cherry Creek ditch and the Platte ditch, which, when completed, will give facilities for washing to hundreds of miners; and the Georgia ditch company have completed a small ditch across a band of the Platte River, and with a "tom" got about an ounce of gold in one day.

The news reports too much snow and ice yet in the mountains to operate to any advantage, and the accounts from prospecting parties are very conflicting.

The Jones stages sent out from Leavenworth by Jones and Russell made the trip back from Denver City in 10 days, leaving May 10th, and arriving on the 20th, without the slightest accident. The Leavenworth times says the news is of the most cheering character and the mines are turning out better than was dreamed of, and it is estimated that nearly $5,000 in dust was brought in to consign to various parties.

A panic seems to have seized many of the immigrants newly arrived at the mines and those in route. A letter from Denver City, May 10th, to the St Louis Democrat, state the number of arrivals is still large, with the tide seems to be equally strong in the homeward bound direction. Many of the returning go by skiff's, dugouts, &c., down the Platte. Some fifty boats carry four or five persons each, had left during the week. The writer says: it is estimated that 2,500 persons have left here for home in the last 20 days. This is an addition to those who turn back before reaching here, induced by the intelligence received from others on the return. Probably as many more reached here in that time; but I think there are no more people in the whole mining country today than there were on my arrival here a month ago. The towns (or villages) which they all are, and small ones too,) seem quite deserted by whites, and as many Indians as pale faces are now in and about this village.

St. Joseph letter of the 21st to the Democrat, give the following account of the return minors in mining reports:

The steamer Hesperian came down today from Omaha with 500 returning gold seekers, and they represent the same deplorable condition of the immigrants that I wrote you up last week. There is considerable uneasiness in those border towns lest these destitute and desperate men commit violence.

Arrivals here today from the mines confirm favorable reports. Statements from parties who have actually been in the mining region are quite flattering, while those who have only been to Kearny, got discouraged and returned, until now the returning tide seems as great as was the outgoing throng six weeks ago.

Misery, starvation, suffering, and death among immigrants on Smoky Hill route almost incredible. The Denver City letter to the Democrat record as follows:

We have had sickening rumors for a week past of horrible suffering from freezing, starvation and robbery of immigrants by way of the Smoky Hill route. Several intelligent gentleman who have arrived by that route, told me they themselves were so long on the way — over sand and hills, and without a road at all, but they were reduced almost to starvation — lived 10 to 14 days upon prickly pears and such few wild onions and other edibles as they could pick up, and also they helped bury several persons who died from starvation. The agent of the stage company brought us in words that he picked up a starving man some 50 miles from here, (an Arrapahoe Indian brought him into the stage line.) Who had come across from the Smoky Hill route (which his company has started on, and tried to follow); that when found he was in a most wretched condition and reduced to a mere skeleton from starvation. His name is Blue, and he is from Whiteside County, Illinois. There were three brothers of them — first, one died, and the two remaining ate from his body, after they've been reduced senseless from emaciation. The second brother died and was nearly eaten up by the survivor. The stage agent went out and buried the remains of the second or the youngest of the brothers, but could not find the remains of the first, who had died. A man named Gibbs was the leader of the starved company. Gibbs got in, nearly starved, and supposes the rest, some nine in all, perished. The survivor was left at one of the mail stations, and the report is confirmed by the stage passengers. Others report large numbers of graves on the route and that many oxen perished and much property been destroyed and abandoned on the way. I saw one party which lost seven out of a train of sixteen oxen.

A letter from one of the stage company to the *Leavenworth Times* represents the man rescued by them as but a shadow. They found the remains of the last brother he had eaten, and buried them. The bones were not perfectly clean, and the brains were taken from the skull. The letter dated Denver City May 8th says:

I have seen a man named Thompson, who came the same route and who live 12 days of on prickly pears and wild onions. He too is a mere walking skeleton. There are others here too who, for three weeks had nothing to sustain them but one hawk and the remnants of a dead ox, whose bones the wolves had almost entirely cleaned.

A lady and gentleman from Leavenworth City informed us that on the road — the same road — in one camp there were lying dead, wrapped in their blankets, five human beings. This is indeed horrible, but not in the slightest exaggerated.

There are many other instances of equally is heart-rending. Those who took the Platte have been more fortunate, generally getting in looking well, except in the wear and tear of the trip, which was, in most cases very long.

Cleveland Daily Leader **(Cleveland, Ohio) 9 Jun 1859.** — Even the Leavenworth Times give that up— that paper, which has done so much to fire up the gold fever and keep the excitement boiling, in its issue of June 3d publishers letters from Denver City to May 22d, and says the "news is very unfavorable and perfectly reliable. We fear the mines are proven to be unremunerative.   It is understood that the express line will dispatch no more coaches for the present. Immigration is all from, and not to the mines."

The third express coach arrived from Denver June.2d, with four passengers but no gold. C. Davison, sent out to the mines as special correspondents for some of the leading papers, was one of the passengers. He brought unfavorable intelligence in both regard of the gold deposits and the agricultural resources of the country. Little or no gold is being discovered, and the general opinion prevailed that the mine had proven to be a failure. The mining towns nearly forsaken, and half the cabins at Denver City and Auraria were vacant. There's no business of any consequence transaction, and but little coin or gold dust in circulation. Provisions were nearly exhausted and no flour to be had.

The weather up to May 22d had been cold and dreary. But few summer like days, and the night very cool. Trees but partly leaved out, and grass but a few inches high. In the balance of the mountains food for cattle is abundant. South Platte is high and still rising.

Remnants of parties of footmen by way of the Smoky Hill route continue to arrive, who report the loss of many lives by sickness and starvation. The estimate is over 100 dead. Dr. Greenlee, a native of Geauga Co., Ohio, but lately of Iowa Point, died at Denver on the 20th ult., from the effects of billious fever. He was a dentist, came to Denver City last fall, and was much respected.

Two large train from Kansas City to Denver City on the 21st, consisting of over 30 wagons, by the Santa Fe route, in good condition. The newcomers generally left at once for the mountains.

A letter to the St. Joseph Gazette, written from Denver City by William G. Piouts, a brother of the editor, who has been in the mines since last fall, and intends to stay and see the thing through, gives what appears to be an honest account of the mines. He says :—

" I don't think there is a place known here where a man can make or average over $2.50 per day, with a sluice, and by this you can judge how rich the mines are, as I am aware you have had some experience in gold countries. Unless better diggings are found, I think any man who is doing well in the states, will regret the hour he left and came to this country to do better.— I would advise all persons to stay where they are. These mines will never pay a man to work them when provisions are as high as they are here Until farmers come here to settle down and find ready sale for their produce—provisions come down to their proper value, bacon 8 or 9 cents per pound, flour $6 per sack, &c.— then, and not until then, will it pay any man to work."

Vermont Journal (Windsor, Vermont) 11 Jun 1859.

> A late letter from Denver City reports that Captain Basset and John Scudder, emigrants from Massachusetts, though old friends, quarreled on the way out, and Scudder killed Bassett after they reached the mines The murderer was to be hung by the people, but he escaped.

Vermont Journal (Windsor, Vermont) 11 Jun 1859.

Leavenworth Times (Levenworth, KS) 18 June 1859. — **LETTER FROM DENVER CITY** "With an idle moment hanging on my hands let me give you an idea of our Indian surroundings. "The trippings of Aboriginal toes can be witnessed in the vicinity of the wigwams (interspersed among the cabins of our boys) every semi-occasionally — if not oftener.

"The hops — in the literal sense of the word — generally proceed to the heart rending tune of awful uniformity, produced by the vigorous abuse of a drum, and a primitive instrument pretending at a similarity to a flute, and consisting of a perforated barrel of an old musket.

"Dreadful as these semi-terpsichorean exercises and this harmonious accompaniments are to the sensibilities of the ear and eye, they are yet pleasantries when compared with the occasional displays of the vocal powers of our red-skinned citizen that we are treated to almost every evening.

"The general chorus of an old community, would be considered the very perfection of musical achievement when heard simultaneously with the dismal taxations of the throats of the copper skinned artists.

"I would liken the vocal performances of the Indians rather to the shrill cry of an owl: the growling of a dog; the yelling of a prairie wolf, than to anything that may be justly considered as coming under the head of human singing.

"Having the misfortune of living within a few yards of a half dozen wigwams, the quiet nights that bless me are far and few between only. The Arapahoe concerts generally invite the wolf-dogs, the usual appendages of Indian camps, to a sort of vocal rivalry with their masters, and it is often not until after midnight that their joint tortures of my auricles come to a stop.

"Disinclined as I am to make use of profane exclamations, the infernal tunes of the Aborigines with their canine accompaniments often elicit denunciations from my lips that would ...shock any Christian heart that heard them."

The *New Orleans Crescent* (New Orleans, Louisiana) 21 Jun 1859.
— Republican of the 15th says: A long letter is published this morning from our correspondent at Denver City. It is of the very latest date. Taken in connection with the other account, it is full of interest to the whole country, in detailing the question of the existence of gold and profitable quantities in the Pikes Peak region. In a private note, we are told that the express company will soon be able to transport from 30 to $40,000 per week. "Several thousand dollars of gold dust could be forwarded if there were money here to buy it."

We make the following extracts from the letter alluded to above, which is dated Denver City, June 4: Several days ago we were startled by reports of several strikes of vastly rich leads of quartz gold to the North Fork of Clear or Vasquez Creek, a tributary from the northeast of the South Platte. I immediately set out to sound the matter, confound the news for once to be based on reality. A Mr. Gregory of Georgia, and several parties from Indiana, Illinois and Iowa, while prospecting the hilly banks of the above-mentioned stream, have come across a number of streaks of burnt quartz which induce them to use their picks and shovels and pans forthwith. The first pan of surface dirt yielded over four dollars' worth of particles of gold of the finest description; and the digging being carried on deeper through the rock beneath, a lead of rotten quartz, encased in Solid Rock of the species, of a width of about ten, and a height of almost an equal number of inches, was struck, which found to contain large quantities of gold, varying from five to fifteen dollars to the pan. A number of claims were at once staked out by the discoverers, and the working proceeded with by means of whatever imperfect implements they had at command.

Mr. Gregory himself took nearly a thousand dollars out of this claim in less than a week. A party of five from South Bend, Indiana viz,: two brothers Defrees, two brothers Ziegler and one Chess, obtained nearly $3,000 in six days, that is from the 22d to the 28th day ult., at the average rate of $450 a day. As soon as the news of their good fortune reach this and adjoining towns, an unprecedented rush for what has since been baptized the "Gregory Diggings" ensued. Hundreds of prospectors at once commenced overflowing the narrow valley, on the mountainous bordering of which quartz lead was located. A number of them or as lucky as their predecessors, and at the time I arrived there's some six more abundantly yielding leads have been discovered, on which a large number of claims were already taken. Owing to the altitude and the steepness of the location of the leads, their working is carried on with the greatest difficulty only. When I arrived there but two sluices were in operation, and the dirt was brought down on the minor shoulders from the altitude in some instances of over three hundred feet. In a few days, however, some twenty sluices will be run and a number of dirt slides fixed, and the yield per day, which is now about two thousand dollars out of all leads, we'll reach eight or ten thousand. In about three weeks from now you may confidently look for the first heavy shipment of dust from the region.

The Gregory diggings are located about thirty miles due West from Denver City. Yet the mountainous character of the surrounding country renders it necessary to passed over at least 45 miles before reaching the first lead. The leads, as indicated by the burnt surface quartz already mentioned, run in Southwestern and Northwestern directions, and extend for miles. Whether they are gold bearing throughout has of course, not yet been tested. A number of old Californians are at work in the diggings, and proclaim their utmost confidence in the speedy discovery of an abundance of gold, equal to that of the richest valleys of California. Water, grass and fine wood is plentiful near the diggings.

The excitement about the quartz leads is intense. On my way back to this point I met at least two thousand individuals bound in their direction. Denver City and Auraria now look as dull as New England villages on Sabbath day. Everybody joins the general rush.

All of the facts recited in the foregoing I can warrant to be correct. Most of the gold washed out I have weighed with my own hands. Up to the moment of doing this, and examine personally the lead, I had myself the greatest doubt as to the truthfulness of the reports that induced me to undertake the trip. But having seen, I now believe like St, Thomas, and endeavor to promulgate the results of my observations to the columns of your paper.

In a few days I shall undertake a second trip and furnish you with more extensive and detailed data as to the new avenues of wealth dust thrown open to the gold seeking multitude there now congregated in this latitude.

Few, if any of the newcomers from the states have been turning back during the last 10 days. They all make for the mountains.

In conclusion, may I say that Mr. Martin Field, the postmaster of the express company, of late has visited the Jackson diggings, located on the South Fork of Clear Creek, and returns beautiful specimens of nugget gold found in that neighborhood, and that this morning a minor from there with three ounces of gold, consisting of small lumps, the weight of which ranges from two to six pennyweights. The Gregory gold is all but imperceptible to the naked eye, when mixed with dirt, and has to be quick silvered. Provisions of all kinds have been very scarce, and consequently high, up to yesterday, which witness the arrival of the first supply train sent out by Messrs. Russell & Jones, of Leavenworth and Pikes Peak express. It numbers 25 heavily loaded wagons, the contents of which will undoubtedly tend to make the satisfaction of physical wants more easy and less expensive.

The *New Orleans Crescent* (New Orleans, Louisiana) 21 Jun 1859. — The excitement about the Gregory diggings is still on the increase. Authentic information has been received here today of the striking of still richer leads by a prospecting party, conducted by Mr. Gregory, and the sale of the latter's claim on the original Gregory lead for not less than $21,000 to a party of four, of whom three, viz: Amos Gridley, E. B. Henderson, from Cass County Ind., and a Wm. Allen from Fulton County, Illinois, are known. The brothers Defrees, who also had two claims on the Gregory lead, sold their interest for $7,500 and $7,000. One of the Ziggler brothers sold a claim, which he had bought a week previous for $50, for $6,000. A number of other sales of less magnitude are also reported. Marshall Cook, of Douiphan, bought a claim of Gregory for $600, and Samuel J. Jones, a well-known railroad contractor, two of another individual for three mules and $600 cash respectively.

The exodus to the diggings is daily extending in volume. Denver City is all but deserted. I do not think that more than 300 are now living within the limits.

Mr. St. James, a Mexican trader of Scott descent, now domiciled in this place, bought this morning something over 2 ounces of nugget gold, consisting of lump swelling from 2 to 7 pennyweights each. They had been brought in from the Jackson diggings.

The arrivals from the state still continue to be large, but returning immigrants have become a rather scarce article. Whoever lands here now, at once steers for the mountains.

A business correspondent of Smoot, Russell & Co., of Leavenworth, writes the following letter:
DENVER CITY, June 4, 1859.

The *New Orleans Crescent* (New Orleans, Louisiana) 21 Jun 1859.
— I send you today, for Leavenworth City and Pike's Peak Express, gold dust amounting in the value to $403.35, for what you will please give me credit. The package marked is Platte River Gold and worth here $18 per ounce. That marked Jackson & Boulder is also worth $18. This you will observe, is a very fine specimen comment is calculated have a good effective seen by California minors. It resembles California gold more closely than any other yet discovered.

I write you honestly, gentlemen, and it is my firm belief that in two weeks I will be able to ship you as purchasers on consignment from five to ten thousand dollars.

The gold in the largest packages from Gregory and is saved with Quicksilver. For this I paid $16 per ounce. As soon as possible, advise me as to the true value of each specimen.

The mines are surprisingly rich, so old miners say. They are astonished, and cannot believe it, even if they do see it. Claims are being sold every day at from $1 per foot to $20. These are representations made to me by parties in whom I have the most implicit faith.

The holders of the gold district at Gregory's demand $20 per ounce for it. This is too much, and I will not give it unless you so instruct. I am willing to give $16.

Since I wrote you last, the report from the mines continue to grow more encouraging. New leads have been struck and proven to be equally as rich as those about which I advised you in my last. At Gregory's those who have their claims fully open are making from $50 to $100 to the man per day.

View of the Rocky Mountain News building near 1301 Walnut Street in the Auraria neighborhood of Denver, Colorado. Shows a single story wood frame building with brick chimney.[6]

Montgomery, Park County, Colorado, consists of log dwellings; many are under construction. Stumps are in the foreground, and the hillside in the background is covered with bare trees. Founded in 1859, This silver boom town was abandoned by 1868.[7]

Montgomery, Park County, Colorado, consists of log dwellings; many are under construction. Stumps are in the foreground, and the hillside in the background is covered with bare trees. Founded in 1859, This silver boom town was abandoned by 1868.[8]

GREGORY GOLD DIGGINGS, COLORADO, MAY, 1859. Page 181.

Reproduction of ink rendering; shows Gregory Diggings, Central City, Gilpin County, Colorado, with miners panning for gold and a tent reading: "Grocery."[9]

CROSSING THE PLATTE.

Illustrations show scenes relating to the Colorado gold rush including two men, next to a wagon train, on their way to Pike's Peak; a covered wagon with "Pikes Peak" on it; and a wagon train crossing the Platte River, as Indian (?) women sit on the bank, Colorado.[10]

Chapter 3: 1859 July - September

Upon my remarking to a gentleman last Sabbath that the accommodations for church service were rather primitive, he replied "True, but we shall have a large house for religious worship built before next Sunday! Erecting a church in a single week, is in accordance with the prevailing spirit of the country.

-Letter from Colorado, 1859.

Horace Greely in a letter from 'Denver City, June 10th, says that there is gold here but it is harder to get by digging than almost any other way. A few will make fortunes here, while many will loose all, and go away utterly bankrupt.

Delaware Gazette (Delaware, Ohio) 8 Jul 1859.

The Daily Lawrence Republican (Lawrence Kansas) July 14, 1859. — Denver City and Auraria have a joint population of 1,000 and can boast of between three and four hundred houses. About one third of the buildings, however, have never been roofed or 'chinked;' they were commenced last winter for speculative purposes. Two or three of them are farmers; the remainder of hewed pine logs, the chimnies and fireplaces of sun dried earth, and roofs of split logs, covered with prairie grass and plastered over with mud.

"I have seen only two wooden floors, and perhaps twenty glass windows. One thrifty housewife has covered the ground with clean corn sacks, and hanging sheets and table cloths upon the walls has given her mansion quite a luxurious appearance; and another residence, whose mistress must by very aristocratic, actually possesses a cotton carpet, and has two engravings hung upon the walls.

"Chairs are like angels' visits. The furniture consists mainly of stools, benches and bedsteads of home manufacture, and rough boxes, which by such trivial feminine deceptions as cloth covers are made to look quite neat, and impressed into service as dressers, bureaus, cupboards, etc....

"Every description of gaming is carried on openly, a large number of professional gamblers having spent the winter here, and come in with the spring immigration. In the evening they employ musicians to attract the floating population, and their tables are the most popular resorts in town. Hardly a day passes in which they do not bleed some miner or immigrant — and yet players are plenty, and will be while the crop of fools continues unfailing. A driver for the Express Company recently lost $100 at one of their tables in twenty minutes ... and a miner was plucked to the tune of $130 a few nights since. Some of the gamblers are making $100 per day, for weeks in succession.

"Shooting affrays are of so common occurrence that they attract little attention. On Friday, two gamblers, after staking $100 on a game of 'seven up' in which each cheated to the extent of his knowledge, became involved in a quarrel about it, which they were about to settle with pistols and knives, when someone separated them. A few hours after one of them, still under the influence of liquor, entered the crowded saloon and fired six shots at random … Singularly, no one was injured.

"He afterwards entered the room on horseback, leading another steed, and performing various equestrian feats, to the infinite disgust of the visitors. The bar keeper in the same establishment recently had a pistol shot fired into the wall within six inches of his head, and several times within the past week. Such experiences must detract somewhat from the lofty felicity of selling whiskey, even though it commands a quarter a drink.

A LETTER FROM MR. MARKLE.—Through the kindness of Mrs. Markle, we have procured the following abstract of a letter from our late City Recorder, J. W. Markle, Esq., who is seeking his fortune in the Pike's Peak gold regions:

Russell's Diggings, July 10th, 1859.

The *Dubuque Weekly Times* (Dubuque, Iowa) 25 Aug 1859. — I have no doubt but that this will prove to be as good a gold country as ever California was. There is a gulch claim just in front of our tent, from which I have seen washed with one small tom $400 a day, and it continued so for several days, yielding from $275 to $450 per day. — The worth of pieces range from one cent up to $16. We have 26 feet just above him, upon which Goldsberry and myself have been at work this week, and have got one pit opened and one tom running. We know not yet how much we have washed out, as we have not cleaned it up, but can see some fine pieces — one as large as a pea.

As for our mountain lodes, we have abandoned them for this season, as we can do nothing with them until the quartz mills come, which we think will not be this season. We think we have enough of mountain claims from which to make our "pile" next year.

I intended writing to the Times, but the mails are so uncertain — and besides it costs 50 to 60 cents to send a letter out and 55 cents to get one here. Out mail matter is undoubtedly a most clumsily conducted affair. We all thought that we were to have a regular United States mail here, but it seems that Russell & Jones, the express men, have the whole thing yet in their hands, and charge 25 cents per letter from Denver City. When the mail arrives, the letters are not delivered until the names of those they are for are written on a slip of paper, for which five cents extra is charged. Uncle Same should not thus allow his citizens be swindled by these land pirates. 25 cents more is charged to get them to the mountains. I know not what becomes of the papers — probably they never bring them, if they do, a company that will stoop so low as to charge a man five cents for writing his name is mean enough to sell the papers, as they are sold for twenty-five to thirty cents.

Those who intend coming here to sell goods, should come this fall, as they can live very comfortably in Auroria or Denver City during the winter. Those who intend mining should not come before Spring, as by the time they would get here, nothing could be done during the whole winter.

Goldberry and I intend to leave for the States between the 1st and 15th September next. Ed. James will not return this fall, but will stay here and take care of our claims and let me bring out his family in the Spring.

JOHN W. MARKLE.

The Future of the Kansas Gold Region.

In his last letter from Denver City to *The N. Y. Tribune*, Mr. Greeley says:

The Findlay Jeffersonian (Findlay, Ohio) 22 Jul 1859.

The *Tiffin Tribune* (Tiffin, Ohio) 22 Jul 1859.

Belmont Chronicle (Saint Clairsville, Ohio) 28 Jul 1859. — Thousand who rush hither will rush away again, disappointed and disgusted as thousands have already done; and yet the gold is in these mountains, and the right man will gradually unearth it. I shall be mistaken if two or three millions are not taking out this year, and some ten millions in 1860; — though all the time there will be as now, a stream of rash adventures heading away from the diggings, declaring that there is no gold there, or next to none.

Not gold alone, but lead, iron, and (I think) Silver or Cobalt, have already been discovered here and other valuable minerals doubtless will be as the mountains are more thoroughly explored — for as yet they have not been even run over. Those who are now intent on the immediate organization admission of the new state, maybe too fast, yet I believe the Rocky Mountains in their immediate vicinity — say between Fort Laramie on the North, and Taos on the south — will within three years, have a white population of one hundred thousand.

☞ Mr. Greeley concludes a letter from Denver City thus:

Mining is a pursuit akin to hunting and fishing, and, like them, enriches the few at the cost of the many. This region is doubtless pre-ordained to many changes of fortune; to-day giddy with the intoxication of success; to-morrow, in the valley of humiliation. One day, reports will be made on the Missouri by a party of disappointed gold seekers that the 'Rocky Mountain humbug' has exploded and everybody is fleeing to the States who can get away; the next report will represent these diggings as yellow with gold. Neither will be true; yet each in its turn will have a thin substratum of fact for its justification. Each season will see its thousands turn away disappointed, only to give place to other thousands, sanguine and eager as if none had ever failed. Yet I feel a strong conviction that each succeeding month's researches will enlarge the field of mining operations and diminish the difficulties and impediments which now stretch across the gold seeker's path, and that ten year's hence, we shall be just beginning fairly to appreciate and enjoy the treasures now buried in the Rocky Mountains.

The *Morning Democrat* (Davenport, Iowa) 25 Jul 1859.

74

Wisconsin State Journal (Madison, Wisconsin) 25 Jul 1859. —

CHANGES OF THREE WEEKS.

Less than three weeks have passed since I was here with Messrs. Greeley and Villard, but the development during that period has been wonderful. Then there were but twenty sluices in operation, now there are upwards of *three hundred.* They are constructed of lumber which costs from $250 to $300 per thousand, and are therefore substantial evidence that the diggings pay well. They stand as thick as possible for several miles along the little stream which threads this ravine. The number of miners has increased fully three-fold; there are not less than 15,000 persons in these and the adjacent diggings. Houses have gone up with almost inconceivable rapidity. Through the whole day the forests resound with the echo of the chopper's ax and the crash of the falling pine and hemlock some of them majestic trees, 150 feet in height. The number of women here has increased from seven to more than a hundred; a Masonic lodge is established; auction and commission houses are opened; lawyers and physicians' signs begin to appear; a store-room 16 feet by 18, with a ground floor, rents for $40 per month: and a single building lot in this lively settlement has been sold for $500. Upon my remarking to a gentleman last Sabbath that the accommodations for church service were rather primitive, he replied "True, but we shall have a large house for religious worship built before next Sunday! Erecting a church in a single week, is in accordance with the prevailing spirit of the country.

THE DIGGINGS IN THE DAY TIME.

During the day the diggings present a very busy appearance. Early in the morning the water is "turned on" at the upper sluices, and never was stream husbanded with so much care. It must pass through three hundred sluices before it escapes from the net-work of the miners, and be permitted to pursue its unmolested, course toward the Platte. The creek is becoming quite low; and there is some danger that it may fail, which would prove a serious calamity. The springs in which the mountain abounds, could be made partially to supply its place; already there are some pumps in operation. As augers are not found here, they are constructed of boards instead of legs. There are a few diggings in the stream bed; but the "leads" are mostly up the hillsides, several rods from the water. In some instances the dirt is brought down to the sluices in sacks, upon the shoulders of men; but the sacks are usually drawn on rough sleds, or let down by ropes, upon the smooth trunks of pine trees, from which the bark has been peeled — the inclined plane and the railroad in a crude form. the sluice is a large wooden trough, or a series of them, through which a little stream of water is turned. The dirt is shoveled into it, and then stirred with hoes; it is slowly washed away, while the gold, which of course sinks, is retained by slats nailed upon the bottom. Much of it, however, escapes and is wasted with the dirt. The quartz — not yet decomposed — is taken from the sluice and piled up beside it. Awaiting the arrival of crushing machines, to separate the precious metal from the stone. Much of it promises to yield very richly. The sluice-stream does not - wash gold entirely clean; after it has been running all day, and many cords of earth has passed through it, a small quantity — of course very rich — remains in the bottom, to be shoveled into buckets; and. then washed out in pans. I have seen the top of one of these buckets of earth so rich that it seemed as if one could take from it a double hand-full of the glittering flower-gold; though closer inspection would show considerable dirt among it. Even after panning, the gold is not entirely collected; quicksilver is then put in to separate it from, the dirt. The compound which results in turn placed in a retort and heated, to expel the quicksilver; and then the gold remains in mass. This is usually not so valuable as the scale of dust gold, washed out without the aid of quicksilver, but I have been a cake of it, of the shape and nearly the size of a common tea-saucer, which shone clear and beautiful as the finest jewelry. It weighed 510 penny-weights, and was taken out in one day by five men. It is the best day's work I have positively known of, though I hear reports of five men, who in two instances took out a thousand pennyweights in one day. After the dust gold is thoroughly washed, it is often mingled with particles of black sand; but the latter contains so much iron that it is readily taken out with a small magnet. The "rocker" is somewhat like a common cradle, the dirt being separated from the gold by the movement. Few of them are in use here. It is a valuable utensil, but I must confess, a strong preference for the domestic article. The "long Tom" is a modification of the sluice. As I have already stated, the men who are running the sluices generally seem contented; work hard everyday, mind their own business, and do not grumble.

BY NIGHT.

 As evening approached, I took a long ride among the mountains. There are many fine views: fertile spots of prairie, abounding in ver- dure; dark valleys along which one who gazes from the elms above can detect the course of gushing streams, fringed with forest trees; distant ranges and peaks, silvered and softened by a mantle or mist; bare bald mountain-brows, which stand isolated and bad, like aged men who have outlived both cotemporaries and descendants; and little lakes, which nestle among the summits, in the deep; pine woods. Dark ness was just closing over the diggings as I returned and rode down into the valley to view them by night. The view in the diggings, was novel and picturesque, the valley was lighted up by thousands of campfires, casting the shadows of the tall trees in every direction, and throwing a lurid glare upon the swarthy faces of the miners. Some were cooking by their log-fires; some dispatching their evening meal upon the earth or tables of pine-bark, and others sitting upon logs or lying on the ground, smoking and conversing. From one camp issued the lively notes of a violin and banjo; and from another, the tune of

"Home, Sweet Home," floated forth upon the evening air, in a low, plaintive voice, which told that the heart or the singer was with dear ones far away. A narrow, tortuous path, along the side of the hill, at last gave me a fine view of the mountain city. The numerous log building of the settlement were thrown into bold relief by the camp-fires in front; and behind, an almost perpendicular mountain, thickly studded with pines, appeared to rise to the very skies. In another direction the fire was raging upon what seemed an isolated mountain. It crept slowly and evenly up the sides, until, on the summit, it struck a single tree, which was like tinder, when it ran up the trunk and branches with wondrous rapidity, and finally pointed the whole into an almost perfect cone of flame, resting upon a back-ground of mountain and cloud. In a few seconds the striking picture one of Nature's pyrotechnics was broken; and I turned and rode slowly into camp.

> A letter from Pike's Peak says that gambling and whisky-drinking flourish there extensively. Tanglefoot whisky sells for 25 cents a drink, and "it will almost make a man shed his toe nails."

The *Cecil Whig* (Elkton, Maryland) 30 Jul 1859.

☞Horace Greeley, in a letter from Denver City, says that he was informed by a wagoner on the Plains, that the tornadoes were occasionally so severe that there had been "instances of tires being blown of from wagon wheels."

Raftsman's Journal (Clearfield, Pennsylvania) 27 Jul 1859.

KANSAS AFFAIRS.

St. Louis, Aug. 12.—A despatch in the Republican contains dates from Denver City to the 3d inst. A Convention of 166 delegates was in sesaion for the purpose of taking the steps necessary to forming all the country adjacent to the mines into a territory, to be called Jefferson. The intention is to apply to the next session of Congreas for a territorial government.

North Star (Danville, Vermont) 20 Aug 1859.

JEFFERSON TERRITORY.—The Pike's Peakers are taking measures to secure from Congress, at the next session, an organization for the Territory of Jefferson, in accordance, we suppose, with the bill for that purpose reported by Mr. Stevens last winter. An additional reason for this action is found in the omission of the Western part of Kansas from the area of the State, as its limits are fixed by the Wyandotte Constitution. Of all the proposed territorial organizations, this has the most substantial merits. The population of the Pike's Peak region is undoubtedly much greater than that of Arizona, Nevada, or Dacotah, and its prospects of speedily becoming a prosperous State, are certainly equally as good. We trust however, that Congress will be in no hurry to increase the number of these petty subordinate Commonwealths, to be constant subjects of agitation and controversy for the whole country.—*Cin. Gazette.*

White Cloud Kansas Chief (White Cloud, Kansas) 8 Sep 1859.

FROM DENVER CITY. — *Leavenworth, Sept.* 17. — Advices from Denver city to the 8th have reached here. The returns from that district give a majority of 933 against the State Constitution and in favor of the Territorial organization. The returns from the mountain districts had not been received.

A large number of miners were leaving the mountains for the valleys, in consequence of the prevalence of rain and snow storms.

The *National Era*

(Washington, District of Columbia) 22 Sep 1859.

Results of Pike's Peak Gold Digging.

A Denver City letter of Sept. 15th, gives some facts and figures showing the progress in working the gold mines. The receipts of *dust* by the mercantile communities of Denver and Auraria from June 1st to Sept. 15th, figure up $72,985; nearly all received since the discovery of the Gregory diggings.

The letter also notices some of the pickings up of a few industrious as well as lucky fellows:

Cleveland Daily Leader (Cleveland, Ohio) 30 Sep 1859. — On last Wednesday the famous Georgian, John H. Gregory, embarked for his former home in Dawson County, Ga. He carries the comfortable little sum of twenty-five thousand dollars in dust with him — the result of his mining operations since the memorable 13th of May, the day on which be made his lucky strike in the valley now bearing his name.

A few days ago an individual by the name John Steiner, formerly of Jefferson Co., Wis, returned from the Russell Gulch, after having mined last ten weeks, he had around him a belt containing over four thousand dollars in gulch gold.

Another equally lucky gold hunter returns on the coach that will bring you these lines. His name is Benjamin Barrows, and he hails from Eastern Kansas. He came here not more than four months ago in an entirely destitute and trapped condition, a member of the generally ill-fated hand cart fraternity. He is said to have made his appearance on Cherry Creek, with just one shirt, a pair of inexpressibles torn into shreds and a shirt ditto. He now goes home loaded with five thousand dollars worth of gulch gold. In addition to Mr. Barrows' gold, the Express coach is freighted with $18,000 more, $8,000 of which belong to another passenger, Mr. Murphy, of the firm of Wallingford 4 Murphy, of this place. The balance shipped by the Express Company on their own and others account.

Chapter 4: 1859 October –December

"If the citizens of Auraria are desirous of saving the good reputation of their town, let them be aroused from their present indifference, and sweep the Augean stables without delay."

-

Letter from Colorado, 1859

Later from the Kansas Mines.

The Pike's Peak Express which left Denver City on the 22d ult. arrived at Leavenworth on the 30th. The Mountain City Gold Reporter of the 17th has the following :

The mines are being very energetically worked and more gold is being taken out weekly than at any time this season.

Messrs. Cotton & Co., on the Cotton Lode, on Prospect Hill, are making about $12 a day to the hand. They have to wash in a small gulch that only affords water to wash half the day.

Messrs. Kyle & Co. inform us that they have made $10 per day to hand since June.

Messre. Baker & Co. washed two pans of dirt on Saturday last ; from one they got $6, from the other $6 50 ; their claim is about three hundred feet west of the Bates Lode.

Mr. Thos. B. Price informs us that Saturday last three men on his claim, in dry diggings near Chicago Creek, took out 157 pennyweights.

Messrs. Burgher, Myers & Co., whom we reported last week as making $3 to the hand, are now making from $8 to $10 ; they took out a handsome nugget on Monday weighing 23 dwt.

The *New Orleans Crescent* (New Orleans, Louisiana) 10 Oct 1859.

The *New Orleans Crescent* (New Orleans, Louisiana) 10 Oct 1859.
— Fights rows, brawls, shooting and stabbing, affrays are the order of the day. The frequency of blood collisions on the other side of the Creek, where mat of the gambling saloons are located, has become fearful. A crisis is evidently approaching, in consequence of the intolerable boldness with which law and order are at present defiled in that quarter. The Vigilance Committee will doubtless step in before long and submit the foul atmosphere of that locality to a thorough purification. If the citizens of Auraria are desirous of saving the good reputation of their town, let them be aroused from their present indifference, and sweep the Augean stables without delay.

The election returns are now complete. A majority of nearly three thousand is figured up against the Constitution, and that piece of folly is thus finally and fortunately disposed of. A second Oxford has loomed up in this region. A mystic locality by the name of Fountain City, has returned nearly eleven hundred votes. The true number of the votes then and there called would probably be obtained by cutting of two figures to the right.

A somewhat lively business has been done of late in the line of politics. Q uite a number of candidate for the Delegateship to Congress have made their appearance. Among these, Gen. Larimer and B. D. Williams, late Superintendent of the Express Company, figure prominently. A sort of nominating Convention was to be holden yesterday at Golden City, the result of which has, however, thus far failed to transpire. Denver city is not represented in it. It is more than probable that most of the candidates now announced will run independently of the action of any conventional body, and I should not be surprised if half a dozen individuals, claiming to represent the people of the gold region, should appear in Washington City in December next, and claim admission. The election of a delegate itself is to come off on the first Monday in October. Party issues have not thus far been raised between the several aspirants to the honor, and perhaps, profits of a Delegataship. The only difference of opinion between them seems to consist in the higher or lower degree of enthusiasm they display with regard to the future of this country.

On the 14th inst., Mr. John Steiner, of Westmoreland county, Pa., an old steamboat institution, (the same person whom I mentioned in my last as one of the lucky miners, he having realized about $5000 worth of gold in less than eleven weeks) departed down the South Platte in a sort of flat bottomed scow, for the purpose of taking soundings, etc, with a view of running a light draught steamboat up to this point or the lower crossing. Mr. Steiner is full of confidence in his object to do so. A large band or Arapahoes returned the latter part of last week from an extensive and protracted hunting expedition into the buffalo country. They do not appear to have realised much in the way of meat, hides, furs. etc., during their long absence. Left Hand and Little Horse, their two chiefs, contend that a most fatal disease is raging among the buffaloes, which covers the plains with ten thousands of carcasses, and is so contagious that it is even dangerous to eat the meat of those that were killed by their people.

In consequence of this fatality and the failure—at least the two chiefs assert —to obtain their usual annual presents at the hands of their agent, (Col. Bent, from the Arkansas) great destitution prevails among the red skins, which forced them to appeal to the charitable disposition of their white friends. A "talk" was held with the principal warriors of the hand by the leading citizen, of Denver on the subject, which resulted in the raising subscription for the benefit of the "poor Indians." On Sunday morning, nearly a hundred dollars worth of provisions were distributed among and received by them with visible delight.

Mr. Frank Kershaw returned on Sunday morning last, from the head waters of the Blue River, a tributary of the Colorado of the West, after an absence of nearly a month. He says that over five hundred miners are at work in that vicinity, turning the stream, panning, etc.

He has found prospects as high as from 10c, to $1.60 to the pan. He thinks that next year as much mining will be done on the other side of the range as on this side, the miners had built a large and strong fort, to protect their persons and property from the Utahs. Mr. Kershaw has already taken the back track for the new diggings.

The *New Orleans Crescent* (New Orleans, Louisiana) 10 Oct 1859. —Mr. D. L. Witcher of Richland, Iowa, arrived in this city on Friday, direct from the mines, in fourteen days and eighteen hours. He came through with a single team, and reports the route in excellent condition. The Platte river is very low, and he found no difficulty in fording it. Mr. W. is an old California miner, having worked in the Pacific mines in 1849. He reports his experience, and that of every other California miner, as entirely valueless in the diggings on the eastern slope. He is quite enthusiastic in his opinion of the new diggings, and brings about a $1000 in dust (The product of two months labor.) as a substantial evidence of success. He thinks these mines far richer than those of California, but more difficult to wash. Four quarts mills were in operation when he left, but they were rough, uncouth concerns and did not amount to much. It was getting quite cold in the mountains, and snow was beginning to fall. Mr. W. has a claim on the Mammoth Load near Gregory's Diggings, and will return in the spring.

Later from Denver City.

LEAVENWORTH. K. T., November 5.—The Overland express from Denver City arrived here last night, bringing advices to the 28th ult., and $7,000 in gold dust on consignment, besides $23,000 in the hands of the passengers.

The weather at the mines had been unusually favorable.

An election had been held for officers under the Provisional Government. The result was not definitely known, but as far as ascertained Steel had a majority for Governor.

Efforts were being made to induce the people to participate in the election of a delegate to Congress from Kansas, which takes place on the 8th instant, but the project was opposed by the local papers, which argue in favor of non-intervention in Kansas affairs, having but recently elected a delegate of their own, who is expected to urge the immediate organization of the territory.

The *Daily Exchange* (Baltimore, Maryland) 7 Nov 1859.

From Denver City.

ST. LOUIS, Nov. 28.—The Express from Denver City, with dates to the 17th inst., and treasure amounting to $6,000, reached Leavenworth City on the 25th.

The Provisional Government of Jefferson Territory was working harmoniously. The Legislature was engaged in perfecting a code of laws and concerting measures to raise a revenue to carry on the government.

Mining operations contiue to be prosecuted to a considerable extent, the weather having been more favorable than was anticipated.

The *Star and Enterprise* (Newville, Pennsylvania) 1 Dec 1859.

Yield of the Mines.

A Denver City letter of Dec. 15th to the Missouri Democrat states that it has been estimated by parties who have a good right to know, that there must have been no less than two millions, two hundred and fifty thousand dollars worth of gold taken out of all the various sections of the Pike's Peak mines, by all parties, during the past twelve months. During the Fall months, not less than $37,500 were taken out each week in Russell's gulch alone, as recorded by the Register of those diggings. A yield of two millions and a quarter is a good beginning for young Jefferson.

Cleveland Daily Leader (Cleveland, Ohio) 31 Dec 1859.

Thanks for reading.

Your reviews on Amazon.com and

Goodreads are appreciated.

Index

Notes

[1] [Photograph X-11118], photograph, Date 1859-1868?; {http:// http://bit.ly/2JI7RBP: ac-cessed May 15, 2019), Denver Public Library; crediting Denver Public Library Digital Collections.

[2] [Map CG4311 .P25 1859 .B3], Map, Date 1859; {http:// http:///bit.ly/2KdCfDA: ac-cessed May 15, 2019), Denver Public Library; crediting Denver Public Library Digital Col-lections.

[3] [Map Golbez], Map, Date 1859; { https://commons.wiki-media.org/wiki/File:United_States_Central_change_1859-11-07.png#file), https://creativecommons.org/licenses/by-sa/4.0/legalcode: accessed May 15, 2019), Wikimedia Commons; crediting Golbez.

[4] "$11 10" is the description in the text

[5] So the history here is the tall tales which enticed people to come west.

[6] [Photograph X-28847], photograph, Date 1859; {http://bit.ly/2Me1Mit: accessed May 15, 2019), Denver Public Library; crediting Denver Public Library Digital Collections.

[7] [Photograph X-11118], photograph, Date 1859-1868?; {http://bit.ly/2wtwBVKt: accessed May 15, 2019), Denver Public Library; crediting Denver Public Library Digital Collections.

[8] [Photograph X-11118], photograph, Date 1859-1868?; {http:// http://bit.ly/2XbNvUh: ac-cessed May 15, 2019), Denver Public Library; crediting Denver Public Library Digital Collections.

[9] [Drawing X-114477], photograph, Date May 1859; {http:// http:// http://bit.ly/2W4upyo: ac-cessed May 15, 2019), Denver Public Library; crediting Denver Public Library Digital Collections.

[10] Bierstadt, Albert, Artist. A Pike's Peaker Crossing the Plains ; Crossing the Platte. Colo-rado, 1859. [New York: Harper & Brothers] Photograph. https://www.loc.gov/item/2003663651/.

The Author

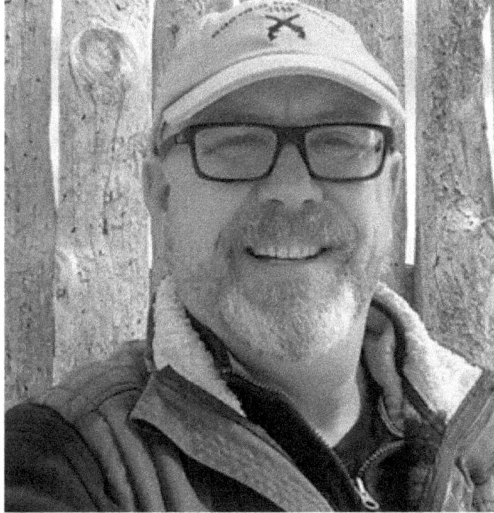

Kent Brooks is the author of "Old Boston: As Wild As They Come," has worked in higher education managing Information Technology and Distance Learning departments for colleges in New Mexico, Oklahoma and Wyoming for more than 20 years.

Growing up in Springfield, Colorado, he listened to southeast Colorado stories about broomcorn, the dust bowl and cowboys of the large cattle companies. He is a long time blogger on various technology topics for his own blog KentBrooks.com as well as the local history blog Bacacountyhistory.com which covers topics about Baca County Colorado, the most southeast county in Colorado. He currently works for Casper College in Casper, Wyoming.

www.ingramcontent.com/pod-product-compliance
Lightning Source LLC
Chambersburg PA
CBHW071454070426
42452CB00039B/1359